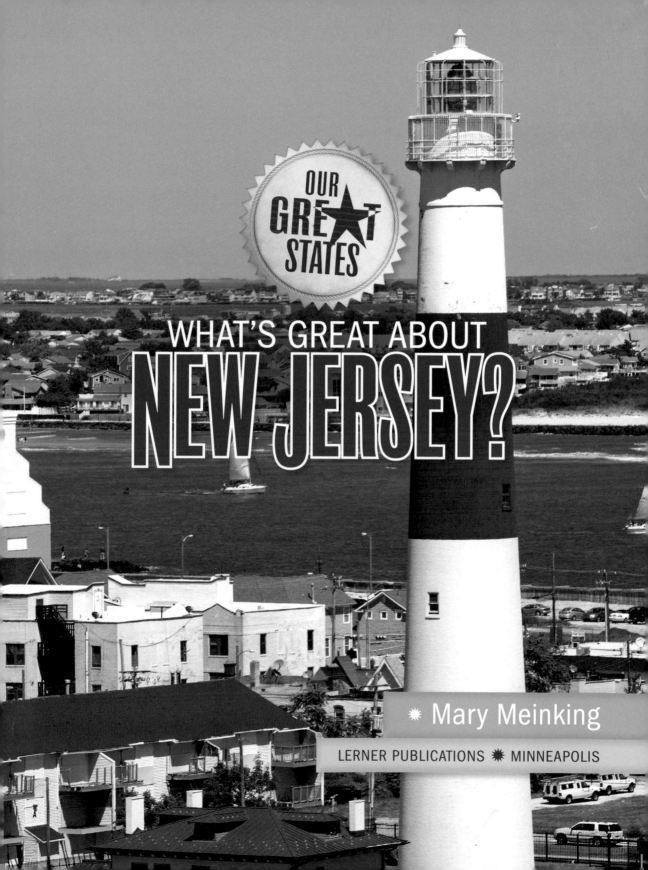

OUR GRE★T STATES

WHAT'S GREAT ABOUT
NEW JERSEY?

★ Mary Meinking

LERNER PUBLICATIONS ★ MINNEAPOLIS

CONTENTS

NEW JERSEY WELCOMES YOU! ✳ 4

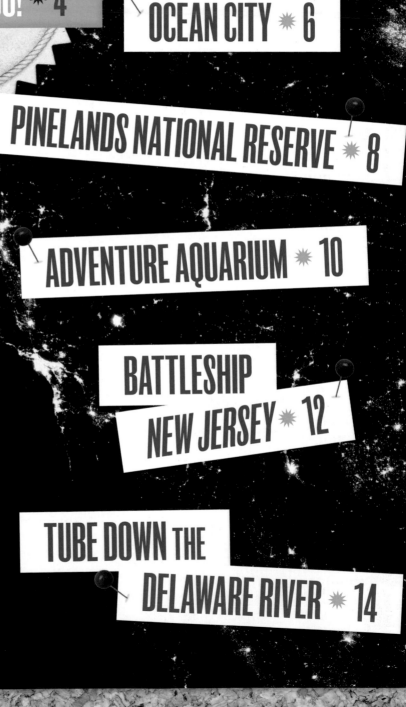

Copyright © 2016
by Lerner Publishing Group, Inc.

Content Consultant: Chris Rasmussen,
Associate Professor, Fairleigh Dickinson
University

Lerner Publications Company
A division of Lerner Publishing Group, Inc.
241 First Avenue North
Minneapolis, MN 55401 USA

For reading levels and more information, look
up this title at www.lernerbooks.com.

Main body text set in ITC Franklin Gothic Std
Book Condensed 12/15.
Typeface provided by Adobe Systems.

Library of Congress Cataloging-in-Publication
Data

Meinking, Mary.
    What's great about New Jersey? / by
Mary Meinking.
        pages   cm. — (Our great states)
Audience: Ages 7–11
    ISBN 978-1-4677-3873-6 (lb: alk
paper)
    ISBN 978-1-4677-8513-6 (pb : alk.
paper)
    ISBN 978-1-4677-8514-3 (EB pdf)
    1. New Jersey–Juvenile literature. I. Title.
F134.3.M45 2015
974.9–dc23   2014047468

Manufactured in the United States of America
1 – PC – 7/15/15

NEW JERSEY Welcomes You!

New Jersey is filled with history and natural beauty. Hike and explore the state's parks and trails. Or relax and float down the Delaware River on a tube on a warm summer day. If you like history, go back in time at the Thomas Edison National Historical Park. Or learn more about the nineteenth century at Historic Cold Spring Village. Look for animals and insects as you tour New Jersey's museums. There is something for everyone in New Jersey. Keep reading to learn about the top ten things that make this state great!

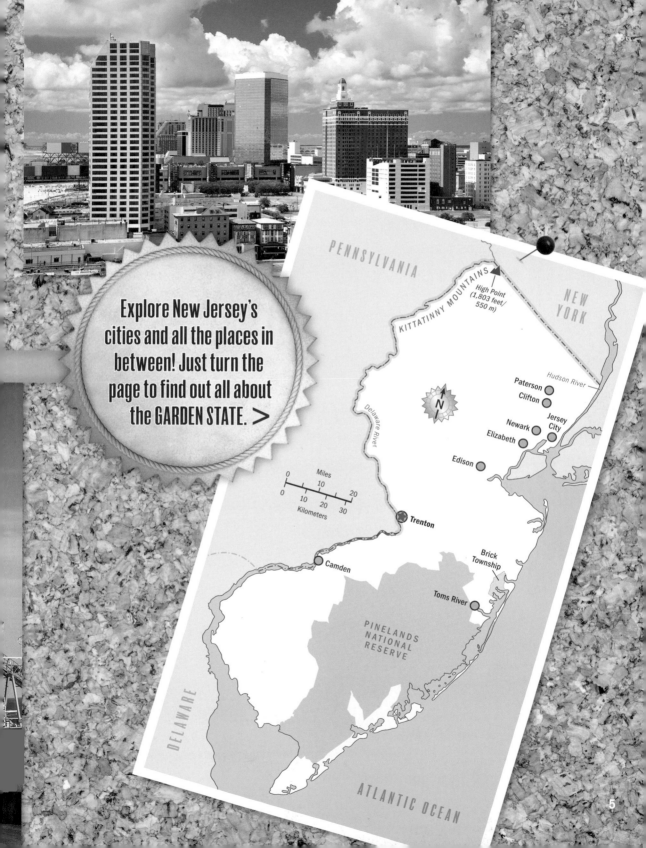

Explore New Jersey's cities and all the places in between! Just turn the page to find out all about the GARDEN STATE. >

PENNSYLVANIA

NEW YORK

KITTATINNY MOUNTAINS

High Point (1,803 feet/ 550 m)

Hudson River

Delaware River

Paterson

Clifton

Newark

Jersey City

Elizabeth

Edison

Miles
0
10
20
0
10
20
30
Kilometers

Trenton

Camden

Brick Township

Toms River

PINELANDS NATIONAL RESERVE

DELAWARE

ATLANTIC OCEAN

OCEAN CITY

> There are few things better than digging your toes into the warm summer sand. New Jersey has 127 miles (204 kilometers) of shore along the Atlantic Ocean. Enjoy the sand and sun at one of the beaches in Ocean City. Here you can swim, make sandcastles, or relax on the beach.

When you need a break from the sand, walk the city's famous boardwalk. Take a spin on the rides at one of two amusement parks. Or maybe you'd like to see a movie or play a game of mini golf. When you're ready for a treat, try fudge, saltwater taffy, or ice cream at one of the many restaurants.

Each Thursday in July and August is family night on the boardwalk. Get your face painted with different designs. Listen to music or watch a magician do tricks.

Ocean City also has guided nature walks in the summer months. You'll learn about seashells, wildlife, and plants on the one-hour trip.

How many seashells can you find on your nature walk?

A variety of tasty snacks are available along Ocean City's 2.5-mile (4 km) boardwalk.

7

PINELANDS
NATIONAL RESERVE

> Southern New Jersey is home to a gigantic forest called the Pinelands National Reserve. It covers 22 percent of the state. The region has sandy soil, swamps, and pine and oak trees. You can explore the forest by hiking, biking, canoeing, or kayaking. Pick your favorite! There are many trails to choose from.

After exploring the trails, visit Batsto Village in Hammonton. Soldiers made supplies here during the Revolutionary War (1775–1783). Visit the General Store to see what early Americans bought. Then make your way to one of the oldest working post offices in the United States. It opened in 1852. If you're visiting Batsto on a weekend, see the blacksmith hard at work.

In October, attend the Pine Barrens Jamboree in Waretown. Listen to country, bluegrass, and folk music. You can pet reptiles that live in the Pinelands. Or see goats, chickens, and horses in the farm animal area. End your day by learning how to start a campfire or build a hut.

Explore one of the Pinelands' many bogs, swamps, and wetlands.

LENAPE AMERICAN INDIANS

American Indians lived in New Jersey for more than ten thousand years before Europeans arrived. Europeans began settling in the area in the 1620s. They traded the Lenape American Indians knives and beads in exchange for furs and land. This contact with Europeans exposed the Lenape to new diseases. Many Lenape died from these illnesses.

ADVENTURE AQUARIUM

> Make your next stop Adventure Aquarium in Camden. You'll see more than eighty-five hundred marine animals, including sea turtles, penguins, octopuses, and seahorses. Don't miss the Penguin Feed and Talk. See how many fish a penguin can eat.

If you like sharks, check out the Shark Tunnel and Shark Den. You'll see more than twenty-five types of sharks. Some of them are more than 10 feet (3 meters) long! Can you spot the great hammerhead shark? Adventure Aquarium is the only US aquarium that is home to this species.

Next, make your way to Hippo Haven. No other aquarium in the world has hippos. Watch the hippos do tricks and eat treats during the Hippo Feed and Talk.

Before you leave, stop at the touch pools. Find out what a shark, a stingray, a sea cucumber, and a sea star feel like. Learn more about sea life at the 4D Theater. Sit back and watch a short movie about different animals.

Lucky visitors will see baby penguins at the Adventure Aquarium.

Meet Button and Genny as they swim past you at Hippo Haven.

BATTLESHIP *NEW JERSEY*

> While in Camden, visit Battleship *New Jersey*. The warship was active from World War II (1939–1945) through the Persian Gulf War (1990–1991).

Visitors can tour the almost 887-foot-long (270 m) ship. Check out the upper and lower sections. Use an audio device and a headset to listen to former crew members talk about each room as you walk through. See the bridge, the communications room, and the officers' cabins. You'll get the chance to climb ladders and walk through passageways.

After touring the ship, take part in an overnight encampment program. Feel what it's like to be a US Navy sailor. You'll sleep in the crew's bunks, eat in the mess hall, and climb into the seat of the 16-inch (41-centimeter) gun turrets. You can buy dog tags to remember your visit.

See the communications room (*left*) and the mess hall (*above*) on your tour of Battleship *New Jersey*.

TUBE DOWN THE DELAWARE RIVER

> If you're looking to cool off from the summer heat, make a trip to the Delaware River. Bring your own tube or visit Delaware River Tubing in Frenchtown. Choose from single, double, or triple tubes. Strap many tubes together for your group to float as one unit. Then sit back and enjoy your three- to four-hour trip.

If you'd rather go faster, rent a canoe, a raft, or a kayak. Pick two more people to join you in a canoe. Or fit up to four people in a raft. You can choose from a few different kayaks.

Stop halfway down the river to enjoy a barbecue lunch at the Famous River Hot Dog Man. It's free if you are on a Delaware River Tubing trip. Eat your meal at one of the picnic tables in the shallow water.

Put on your life jacket and grab your paddle to make your way down the 6-mile (10 km) stretch of the Delaware River.

THE GARDEN STATE

New Jersey became known as the Garden State because its weather is great for growing crops. It also got its name because farms in the state supplied food for people in New York and Pennsylvania. Workers transported the produce to factories where it was canned and shipped around the world. This created many jobs for New Jersey residents.

THOMAS EDISON
NATIONAL HISTORICAL PARK

> Step back in time by touring the lab of one of the United States' greatest inventors, Thomas Edison. Visit the Thomas Edison National Historical Park in West Orange, where Edison and his team of scientists worked.

Tour the Laboratory Complex first. You'll watch a twenty-minute movie about Edison's inventions before seeing the rest of the building. Explore all three floors of the laboratory. You'll see Edison's library and the cot where he slept between projects. Be sure to tour the Chemistry Lab too. You can see some of Edison's inventions, such as the phonograph.

Nearby is Edison's home. Take a thirty-minute guided tour. You'll learn more about Edison and the history of the home. See all twenty-nine rooms in the mansion, then tour the beautiful grounds. Find Edison's thought bench where he dreamt up many of his inventions.

You can see the heavy machine shop in the Laboratory Complex.

EDISON'S INVENTIONS

Thomas Edison's inventions changed the world forever. The most famous of his inventions include motion pictures and the electric light. Edison did not create the first lightbulbs, but he made them safer and less expensive for homes. He also invented a system to bring electricity into homes.

BARNEGAT LIGHTHOUSE STATE PARK

> Make your next stop in New Jersey the famous Barnegat Lighthouse on Long Beach Island. This red-and-white brick lighthouse is one of eleven lighthouses open to the public in New Jersey. It was first used in 1859. You can climb the 217 steps to the top of this 172-foot-tall (52 m) tower. Catch your breath at the top and enjoy views of the beach and the ocean.

Once you're back on solid ground, walk through the Interpretive Center. You'll learn about lighthouse history and technology. You can also read about former lighthouse keepers and see their pictures.

Explore the seaside forest and walk the 1,056-foot (322 m) trail. Watch for migrating birds. This is an important resting and feeding area for them. Pack a picnic lunch to eat at the park, or get your fishing gear ready. See if you can catch any saltwater fish, such as bass or flounder.

Look for the black bellies of the Dunlin, one of many birds that migrate through New Jersey.

INSECTROPOLIS

> Discover bugs from around the world at Insectropolis in Toms River. Here you'll see thousands of strange insects. Visit exhibits, play games, and see bugs up close.

Start your day at Bug University to learn all the bug basics. Play a few games to see how bugs get their names. Then learn more about the food web. You may even see a beetle eating a small fish! Check out the Rock State Prison exhibit to find out more about bad bugs. These bugs are called pests.

Check out the ant colony to see how ants work together. You can study an anthill chart to see how work is divided. Then watch the live carpenter ants to see what they are working on. Crawl through human-sized termite mud tubes to see what is happening underground.

No visit to Insectropolis is complete without seeing and touching the insects. Two or three times a day, the staff will let you touch or hold a tarantula, a scorpion, a millipede, or a cockroach.

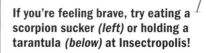

If you're feeling brave, try eating a scorpion sucker *(left)* or holding a tarantula *(below)* at Insectropolis!

MONMOUTH BATTLEFIELD STATE PARK

> Monmouth Battlefield State Park in Manalapan is where one of the largest Revolutionary War battles took place. Stop by the visitor's center to see uniforms, maps, and weapons found on the battlefield.

If you're visiting in late June, join the annual battle reenactment. Soldiers in costumes re-create the 1778 battle. Watch the soldiers relax at their camps, practice their drumming, or perform battle drills. If you'd like to join, pick up a wooden musket and start practicing. You'll also see costumed women cook, sew, and wash for the armies.

After visiting the battlefield, make the short drive to Battleview Orchards in Freehold. From May to October, you can pick strawberries, sour cherries, peaches, apples, and pumpkins. Before leaving, stop in the Country Store for a snack. Enjoy fresh pies, apple cider, doughnuts, or breads.

Don't miss soldiers firing a cannon at Monmouth Battlefield State Park.

GEORGE WASHINGTON

General George Washington spent much of his time in New Jersey during the Revolutionary War. In December 1776, Washington and his troops crossed the icy Delaware River and marched to Trenton. There they surprised British troops and took more than eight hundred prisoners. Most of the bullets used by Washington's troops were made from New Jersey iron. And New Jersey farms provided food for these soldiers.

See all the goods available to buy in the village store.

HISTORIC
COLD SPRING VILLAGE

> Take a trip into the past at the Historic Cold Spring Village outside Cape May. This living history village is open all summer. Wander through the twenty-six remodeled historic buildings. Inside you'll see people in historic clothing hard at work. You can watch a woman spinning wool. Or see a blacksmith repairing a wagon wheel. If you're lucky, you can help the workers with their jobs. Stop at the schoolhouse and see how students learned. Then visit the farm. How many animals do you count?

Visit the village's family area to try on clothing from the nineteenth century. You also can make crafts and play games. Then relax on your horse-drawn carriage ride around the village. End your visit to the village with a treat at the ice cream parlor or the bakery. Then find a souvenir at the Country Store to remember your trip.

Visit the woodworker on your trip to Historic Cold Spring Village.

YOUR TOP TEN!

You have read about ten amazing things to see and do in New Jersey. Now, think about what your New Jersey top ten list would include. What would you like to see if you were to visit the state? Would you want to hike, explore history, or lie on the beach? What activities are most exciting to you? What would you tell your friends to do if they visited New Jersey? Keep these things in mind as you make your own top ten list.

NEW JERSEY BY MAP

> MAP KEY

⭐ Capital city

⭕ City

◉ Point of interest

▲ Highest elevation

–·– State border

Visit www.lerneresource.com to learn more about the state flag of New Jersey.

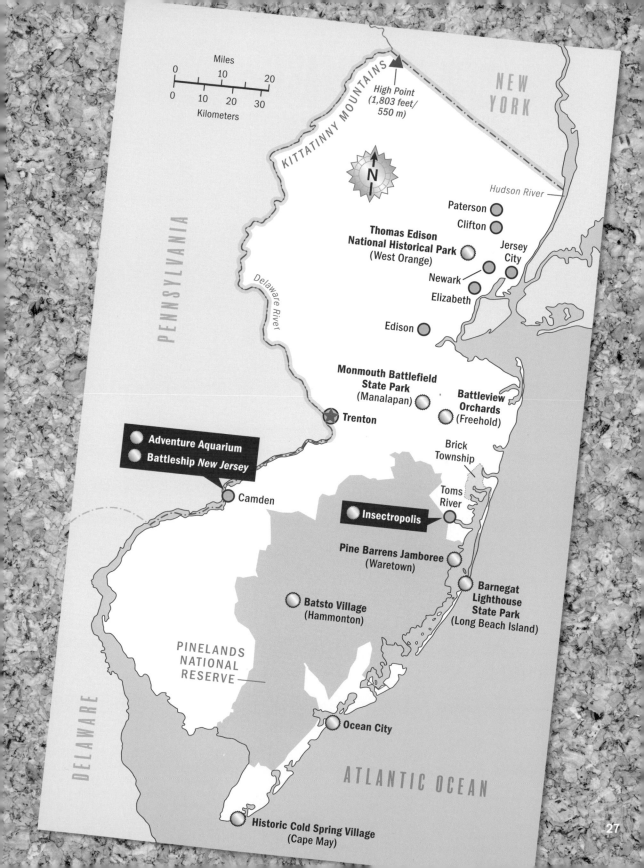

Miles
0   10   20
0 10 20 30
Kilometers

NEW YORK

KITTATINNY MOUNTAINS

High Point
(1,803 feet/
550 m)

Hudson River

N

Paterson ⬤

Clifton ⬤

Thomas Edison
National Historical Park
(West Orange) ⬤

Jersey City ⬤

Newark ⬤

Elizabeth ⬤

Edison ⬤

PENNSYLVANIA

Delaware River

Monmouth Battlefield
State Park
(Manalapan) ⬤

Battleview
Orchards
(Freehold) ⬤

⬤ Trenton

Brick
Township

Adventure Aquarium

Battleship New Jersey

Toms
River

⬤ Insectropolis

⬤ Camden

Pine Barrens Jamboree
(Waretown) ⬤

Barnegat
Lighthouse
State Park
(Long Beach Island) ⬤

⬤ Batsto Village
(Hammonton)

PINELANDS
NATIONAL
RESERVE

DELAWARE

⬤ Ocean City

ATLANTIC OCEAN

⬤ Historic Cold Spring Village
(Cape May)

NEW JERSEY FACTS

NICKNAME: The Garden State

MOTTO: Liberty and Prosperity

> **FLOWER:** common blue violet

TREE: red oak

> **BIRD:** eastern goldfinch

ANIMAL: horse

> **FOOD:** blueberry

DATE AND RANK OF STATEHOOD: December 18, 1787; the 3rd state

> **CAPITAL:** Trenton

AREA: 7,812 square miles (20,233 sq. km)

AVERAGE JANUARY TEMPERATURE: 31°F (–1°C)

AVERAGE JULY TEMPERATURE: 75°F (24°C)

POPULATION AND RANK: 8,899,339; 11th (2013)

MAJOR CITIES AND POPULATIONS: Newark (278,427), Jersey City (257,342), Paterson (145,948), Elizabeth (127,558), Edison (101,450)

NUMBER OF US CONGRESS MEMBERS: 12 representatives, 2 senators

NUMBER OF ELECTORAL VOTES: 14

NATURAL RESOURCES: crushed stone, granite, sand, gravel

AGRICULTURAL PRODUCTS: blueberries, greenhouse and nursery products, horses, milk, peaches, vegetables

MANUFACTURED GOODS: chemicals, computer and electronic products, food products, medical equipment

GLOSSARY

bluegrass: a type of traditional American music that is played on stringed instruments such as banjos and fiddles

boardwalk: a wooden path along a beach

dog tag: a small, thin piece of metal that lists a US soldier's name and other information

encampment: a place where troops set up camp

exhibit: to display something publicly

laboratory: a room or building with special equipment for doing scientific experiments and tests

millipede: a small creature with a long, thin body and many legs

phonograph: an instrument used for re-creating sounds with the vibration of a needle following a groove on a revolving disc

turret: the part on a ship from which guns are fired

LERNER
SOURCE™

Expand learning beyond the printed book. Download free, complementary educational resources for this book from our website, www.lerneresource.com.

FURTHER INFORMATION

Downey, Tika. *New Jersey: The Garden State*. New York: Rosen, 2010. Learn fun facts about New Jersey's symbols, popular attractions, and state history.

Hangout New Jersey
http://nj.gov/hangout_nj
At this jam-packed site, you can play games, learn more about places to visit, and see cartoons.

The Invention Factory
http://www.nps.gov/features/edis/feat001/inventionprocess/ENHS.html
Make your own lightbulb or motion picture while learning fun facts about inventions and Thomas Edison.

Kent, Deborah. *New Jersey*. New York: Scholastic, 2014. This book gives readers a look at some of the state's most popular sites.

New Jersey History Kids
http://www.state.nj.us/state/historykids/NJHistoryKids.htm
Learn more about eleven different places and things that make New Jersey a great state!

Ransom, Candice. *George Washington and the Story of the U.S. Constitution*. Minneapolis: Lerner Publications, 2011. George Washington spent a lot of time in New Jersey. Learn more about the United States' first president.

INDEX

PHOTO ACKNOWLEDGMENTS

The images in this book are used with the permission of: © Aneese/iStockphoto/Thinkstock, p. 1; NASA, pp. 2–3; © Laura Westlund/Independent Picture Service, pp. 5 (bottom), 27; © Jon Bilous/Shutterstock Images, p. 4; © Sean Pavone/Shutterstock Images, p. 5 (top); © omgimages/Thinkstock, pp. 6–7; © Ritu Manoj Jethani/Shutterstock Images, p. 6; © Evlakhov Valeriy/Shutterstock Images, p. 7; Ewan Traveler CC 2.0, pp. 8–9; © Bob Downing/KRT/Newscom, p. 9 (top); Benjamin West, p. 9 (bottom); © Brian Kinney/Shutterstock Images, pp. 10–11; © Avi Steinhardt/Courier-Post/AP Images, p. 11 (top); © National News/Zuma Press/Newscom, p. 11 (bottom); © K. L. Kohn/Shutterstock Images, pp. 12–13, 18–19; Allie Caulfield CC 2.0, p. 13; © Ron S. Buskirk/Alamy, pp. 14–15; Library of Congress, pp. 15 (bottom) (HAER NY,43-SHOOTI,1--3), 17 (bottom) (LC-USZ62-105139), 29 (bottom) (LC-DIG-highsm-18082); © auremar/Shutterstock Images, p. 15 (top); © American Spirit/Shutterstock Images, pp. 16–17; National Park Service, p. 17 (top) © Steven Russell Smith Photos/Shutterstock Images, p. 18; © Erni/Shutterstock Images, p. 19; © Mitsu Yasukawa/Star Ledger/Corbis, pp. 20–21, 21 (left); © Joel Zatz/Alamy, p. 21 (right); © Andrew F. Kazmierski/Shutterstock Images, pp. 22–23, 23 (left); Gilbert Stuart, p. 23 (right) © Jeffrey M. Frank/Shutterstock Images, pp. 24–25; © Michael Ventura/Alamy, pp. 24, 25; © nicoolay/iStockphoto, p. 26; © microcosmos/Shutterstock Images, p. 29 (top); © Paul Reeves Photography/Shutterstock Images, p. 29 (middle left); © Elovich/Shutterstock Images, p. 29 (middle right).

Cover: © iStockphoto.com/rococofoto (Ocean City); © iStockphoto.com/sbonk (lighthouse); © Andrew Kazmierski/Dreamstime.com (reenactment); John Donges/Flickr CC BY-ND 2.0 (aquarium); © Laura Westlund/Independent Picture Service (map); © iStockphoto.com/fpm (seal); © iStockphoto.com/vicm (pushpins); © iStockphoto.com/benz190 (corkboard).